Raspberry Pi

— — — — — ❧❦❧❦❧❦ — — — — —

Raspberry Pi programming for beginners, including Raspberry Pi projects, tips, tricks, and more!

Table of Contents

Introduction

Thank you for taking the time to read this book about the Raspberry Pi.

This book covers the topic of Raspberry Pi and will teach you all about how to use and program your own Pi for a variety of projects! We will begin this book by discussing the different models of the Raspberry Pi, and each of their features.

The primary focus of this book will be on the newest and most complete Raspberry Pi model; the Raspberry Pi 3. You will learn all about how the Raspberry Pi 3 operates, how to get started with it, and all of the basic commands that you will need to know.

Also included in this book are a number of interesting Raspberry Pi projects for you to test out for yourself. This includes doing things such as using your Pi to create a media center, powering a security system with the Pi, and even using the Raspberry Pi to build your very own robot!

This book is perfect for beginners, and will have even the most computer-illiterate person understanding and enjoying the Raspberry Pi in no time at all!

Once again, thanks for choosing this book, I hope you find it to be helpful!

Let's get started...

Chapter 1:

Welcome to Raspberry Pi

Every time you pick up your smartphone, drive your car, order fast food, or program your alarm clock, you are handling an embedded system. An embedded system is a computer system that is embedded into a product, and they work much differently to a general-purpose home computer. They are usually small systems which perform a single task in real-time.

When a user operates a typical home computer, they are guided through an intuitive graphical user interface (GUI) that offers endless amounts of utility, software, and interactivity. These computers manage processing power between multiple tasks, and may slow down when handling a heavy load. The user may also replace the parts of a home computer so that they can keep up with technological advances, and extend the lifetime of their system.

Embedded systems are small computers with light-weight operating systems (OS) that are not meant for user modification or access. A user can not easily add new components to an embedded system, such as a microwave, nor can they directly control its processes. They are usually programmed with custom OS's that carry out processes with undivided attention, working and returning results in real-time speed. All of the functions of a typical embedded system are pre-programmed into their microcontroller during its manufacturing.

A microcontroller is an embedded system that generally features a CPU, timer, RAM, ROM, and input/output (I/O) ports. These tiny computers often act as the heart of an embedded system, executing its programmed functions and controlling the other components of a system, like LED's, motors, and speakers.

Most microcontrollers are pre-programmed at the factory, though some microcontrollers like the Arduino Uno are made to allow the user to easily program and reprogram their microcontroller. They can be applied to electronics and also to computers.

Microcontrollers are often centered in system-on-chip (SoC) computers. SoC computers are small, single-board computers that mount multiple components onto one piece. Embedded systems like these attempt to pack as much computing power as possible onto smaller and smaller frames.

SoC computers are all different and can have many various components. A smartphone SoC would carry a cellular radio, though it may not be equipped with an LED. Most SoC computers are built with ARM processors for their power efficiency, though limited x86 SoC computers are manufactured.

As SoC computers become more and more powerful, they start to infringe on the field of personal computers. The Raspberry Pi is an example of such a computer; it is a single-board machine that offers a GUI and the power to browse the web, play video games, and multi-task. It, unlike typical PC's, also offers general purpose input/output (GPIO) pins for usage in electronics systems, like a microcontroller. In this way, Raspberry Pi is bridging the gap between SoC computers and home PC's.

History of the Raspberry Pi

Before the release of the first Raspberry Pi, it was becoming apparent that Science, Technology, Engineering, and Mathematics (STEM) education was simultaneously becoming more in-demand and less attractive to youth. Mobile phones and tablets had become the default with end-user-friendly interfaces that help them not to worry about the intricacies of computing. It was this trend that inspired a group at the University of Cambridge to develop a rudimentary computer that was as affordable as a single textbook.

To be able to fund the development and distribution of their low-cost computer, the team started The Raspberry Pi Foundation. In addition to endorsing the device, the Foundation helps to promote computer science education in elementary schools worldwide. Thanks to the Raspberry Pi Foundation, the Pi was able to be sold at a low price, and overwhelmingly exceeded the original sales projections.

The first releases of the Raspberry Pi 1, the Model B and the Model A / A, debuted on February 2012 and were offered at just $35, and were expected to sell just 10,000 units over a lifetime. To the shock of the developers, the Pi met huge demand and units had to be put on back order. The Raspberry Pi would go on to become the best-selling British computer ever, just a few years after its birth.

Raspberry Pi Versions and Features

The Raspberry Pi Foundation has released a few varying models of their computer since its original inception, each with different specifications. After the first releases, the Pi 1 Models B, A, and A+, they released improved boards in the coming years. The Model B+ and improved Models A+ and B+ set the standard form of the Raspberry Pi, and the Compute Module and Raspberry Pi Zero followed, offering lower prices for an even smaller computer.

The Compute Module is a small chip that is meant for consumer electronics developers to use as the heart of their machines. The Raspberry Pi Zero is a more user-friendly Pi that promises some fair power but requires some more work setting up. Aside from these two releases, the Raspberry Pi product line has few but important variations.

The original Raspberry Pi 1 models can be seen as the proof of concept, not yet perfected. The Model A+ is the least expensive and smallest single-board computer at just $19.99, and the original, the Model B, was set at $39.99. It set some precedents, such as the Broadcom SoC and ARM-compatible CPU, which would be present in every following iteration. It also outfit all mainline models with HDMI inputs and a 15-pin camera interface connector. All models use an SD or MicroSD card for on-board storage. Models B and B+ came with Ethernet connectivity, but B+ brought more USB ports and GPIO pins at a price of just $29.99.

As the consequent models emerged, they amplified the power rating of the small computers, which all use a 5V MicroUSB power supply, like the ones used for smartphones. The Models A and A+ used less than 300 mA or 1.5W. Then, the RPI2 increased it to 600 – 800 mA.

The Raspberry Pi 2 brought other improvements from the Raspberry Pi 1. It raised the price to $39.99, but included a new ARMv7 quad-core processor and doubled the memory from 512 MB to 1 GB (SDRAM through a Micro SD card, like the B+).

It uses the same GPU as the B+, still comes with an Ethernet port, and packs enhanced power onto the same size board, Broadcom BCM2836. It even comes with four USB ports. You can still use a smartphone charger to power the Raspberry Pi, but the Pi 2 requires just a little more: 650 mA, to work properly.

Soon after, the Raspberry Pi 3 debuted, which would stack even more computing capability onto the same, small board.

What is Raspberry Pi 3?

The Raspberry Pi Foundation has released their strongest successor yet: The Raspberry Pi 3. To supplement schools and to reach the wide market that was suddenly demanding more Pi, the Raspberry Pi 3 was created to be the most user-friendly and powerful iteration. The computer was also built not to replace PC's, but to supplement them. This makes the Pi 3 the most valuable computer to a beginning coder who is not already experienced with using GNU/Linux.

The Raspberry Pi 3 is sold at the same price as the Raspberry Pi 2, yet it promises even more value. The new processor is a 64-bit ARMv8, bringing the speed up to 1.2GHz. It also makes use of a 2.0 - 2.5A power supply.

The most exciting aspect of the newest Raspberry Pi is its on-board Wi-Fi and Bluetooth Low Energy (BLE). A user can easily connect their new Pi to their home Wi-Fi network and

Chapter 1: Welcome to Raspberry Pi

begin learning to program without having too much trouble in getting set up.

The people of the Raspberry Pi Foundation want everybody to be able to easily learn and teach others the ways of computer coding. With that in mind, they have introduced NOOBS, which helps beginning users through the steps of installing an operating system (OS). By plugging in a monitor, keyboard, mouse, a microSD card loaded with NOOBS, and the power supply, a new user will be quickly guided to the desktop and sent on their way.

Raspberry Pi 3 was built to be the core of innovative embedded systems, and even beginning programmers can learn how to build their own machines. Its 40 GPIO pins and serial I/O can now borrow from a 2.5A power supply, and its BLE capabilities make it possible for creators to wirelessly control components.

By default, the Raspberry Pi 3 will utilize Raspbian, which is a Debian GNU/Linux distribution that is optimized for Raspberry Pi 3. Other OS's may be installed and used, of course, including Ubuntu and Windows 10. Users may find specific-purpose OS's to be useful, which can transform your tiny Pi into a dedicated, real-time computer.

Another bonus for new users is the amount of software that comes with the latest version of Raspbian. Before they even have to connect to the internet, a beginning programmer can activate their new Raspberry Pi 3, install Raspbian, and enjoy a wide selection of interactive development environments (IDE's) as well as Python games, an entire office suite, and more.

The Future of Raspberry Pi

The possibilities on the horizon are endless. With the Raspberry Pi 3, anyone can easily put together a machine that is both educational and practical. With their mission in mind, the Raspberry Pi Foundation has been working tirelessly to supply the huge demand for computer and engineering skills education.

It is estimated that 2 - 300,000 boys and girls have been exposed to the Raspberry Pi, creating a generation of children who are learning the basics of computers at a young age. Minecraft: Pi Edition gives children a way to play their favorite game while learning about Python programming at the same time. The Foundation has found that, by just putting the tools in the hands of children, they can really influence the world. As it becomes easier and easier for end-users to become experts, we will see the educational legacy of the Raspberry Pi.

The legacy of the Pi is one that will have a lasting effect on the engineering industry. The creators know that they can help diversify the field and spark potential within disadvantaged youth by making their machines cheap, and through working hard on the available software for the Raspberry Pi. Instead of worrying about building a better product or maximizing their profit, the Raspberry Pi Foundation is confident that they can reach out to a growing audience of learners and improve the world. Do not wait for the latest and greatest Raspberry Pi; the Raspberry Pi 3 will be around for a long time.

Chapter 2:

Possibilities with Pi

The Raspberry Pi has quickly become a popular solution for creators worldwide who want to influence computers, electronics, and the real world. As its primary function, the Raspberry Pi has always excelled at computer education. It is an accessible device that gives average users the tools to take control of their computers and the internet. The newest model even has the power to replace an expensive PC.

Some more advanced computing applications will call for a user's skills in electronics. This is another aspect where the Raspberry Pi shines. With the Pi 3, it has never been easier to link the Raspberry Pi to other devices and machines. In addition to the traditional 40 GPIO pins, the new Bluetooth capabilities allow users to control their computers and their homes remotely.

With a combination of basic computing, networking, and electronics knowledge, a Raspberry Pi user can create devices that will help them explore the beauty of the real world. By purchasing sensors, cameras, and other accessories, a user can assemble inexpensive machines that can track the weather, reveal the secrets of wildlife, and capture images of the world around us, the sky, and even outer space.

Users of Raspberry Pi, GNU/Linux, and Python belong to communities of innovators who will change the world with their control of technology. What else will you create with the Raspberry Pi?

Computer Applications

As stated by the creators of the Raspberry Pi, the tiny computers are excellent companions to any personal computer. In fact, you will need a personal computer to bring the thing to life if you do not have a MicroSD card loaded with an OS. Because of its limited processing power, it can not carry out heavy, general-purpose multitasking. It does however, perform specific tasks very nicely and can be easily programmed to take over a task that may run slowly on a typical PC.

A user that becomes familiar with the Raspberry Pi will inherently begin to learn the ways of GNU/Linux. Because the default OS for the Raspberry Pi is Raspbian, users will be encouraged to learn to move past the desktop GUI and to start controlling their computer through commands. After a while, a Pi user will be very familiar with GNU/Linux and will be comfortable changing and using different operating systems.

In addition, users are also encouraged to learn and use Python, the free programming language that was intended to be the Raspberry Pi default. Python is easy-to-learn, useful, and totally free. This makes Python the ideal language to be endorsed by the Raspberry Pi Foundation. Advanced Pi users will know how to automate and customize their computer experiences with Python code.

The Raspberry Pi and GNU/Linux make it very easy to create and host your own web server, allowing you to host images, video, text, and other media on the World Wide Web. A Pi user can become familiar with Apache, Nginx, or other web server software to get their Pi online. Using Wordpress, a Pi user can even begin to host their own blogging website easily, and quickly.

With efficiently-priced processing speed and its easy-to-use GUI, the Raspberry Pi 3 has the power to stand in as a general-purpose workstation, replacing a conventional PC. Although its specifications are modest compared to full, modern PC's, the Raspberry Pi 3 has the ability to perform most of the same functions as a full PC. If the user does not mind sacrificing some speed, the Pi can make a fine home computer.

The Pi can also function as a portable computer with some ingenuity. By adding on a touch-screen monitor, bringing a Bluetooth keyboard and mouse, and enclosing the Raspberry Pi in an attractive case with a battery, the machine can be converted into a hand-held computer. Depending on the user's requirements, a Raspberry Pi can also perform well as a replacement for a laptop computer.

Electronic Applications

As our physical realm becomes woven more and more tightly with the cyber-network of the Internet, we develop what is known as the Internet of Things (IoT). This is a term that describes the internetworking of the things that we use and see daily, and the ways that their conversations with computers are improved. By embedding sensors, software, and network connectivity into every day objects, we infuse our world with technology and can control and sense things remotely.

Chapter 2: Possibilities with Pi

Each iteration of the Raspberry Pi comes with a number of GPIO pins, one of the product's most innovative additions. GPIO pins are able to do many different things when programmed to behave in a certain way. They can be programmed to deliver or receive signals, and they can be adjusted to transmit different levels of power. By learning about these pins and becoming acquainted with their different functions, one can begin to send signals and control other electronics.

The Raspberry Pi is able to be outfit with different sensors, including the official Raspberry Pi Sense HAT. Adding sensors to your programming projects will give your Raspberry Pi electronic eyes, ears, noses, and other things. The Pi can be used to read the temperature, the atmospheric pressure, and its own motion. These signals can all be used in projects to create new, functional devices.

For advanced users, experimentation and learning the ways of robotics is something that entices many users. It has been demonstrated that one can build remote-controlled and sensor-controlled robots that can carry out tasks, help their creators, or just look cute.

Another exciting function of the Raspberry Pi is its ability to be transformed into the heart of a home theater system. The Raspberry Pi can be modified with a USB sound card that will improve its sound quality, but it also comes equipped with an HDMI port, allowing full 1080p HD display. By installing a Kodi-optimized OS onto the Pi, its computing heart will be equipped to access and display multimedia files with ease.

As well as making it easy to create a great home theater system, the Raspberry Pi can also make a fine controller to transform your home into a smart home. With different security, sensing, and robotic applications, your Pi can power projects that watch over your home, manipulate your thermostat, and even open your garage door remotely. By putting your home onto the Internet of Things, you can astound your guests with your ingenuity and creativity.

Your Raspberry Pi can also help to take care of your pets. With some programming and building, the Raspberry Pi can be configured to remind you to feed your pets, or simply do it by itself.

Real-World Applications

There are many ways in which your Raspberry Pi can teach you not just about the internet, computing, and electronic technology, but about the real world around you as well. For example, the Raspberry Pi Weather Station kit gives users the tools needed to build their Raspberry Pi into a device that senses and records the weather for the user. By using the data retrieved by the device and some creative programming, one can use the weather to control their programming worlds.

It has also been proven that the Raspberry Pi can be useful in wildlife photography. Camera trap devices have been created with the Raspberry Pi hardware and its Camera Module, which has the ability to capture high-definition images in a small package. With a Raspberry Pi wildlife trap, you will be able to see what lurks in the wild, or just around your backyard.

While some Raspberry Pi users have taken their Pi to the great outdoors, others have sent their own devices flying toward space on a mission to capture and send beautiful photos. Documentation and blogs can be found on the internet in which a Raspberry Pi, a camera, and a balloon were combined to send the Pi on an ascension toward the upper reaches of the atmosphere, snapping pictures the whole time.

The Raspberry Pi can also be configured and assembled into an inexpensive 360° camera that will allow the user to take pictures all around them. 360° images and videos are becoming more and more popular, though the technology is still rather expensive. The Raspberry Pi, mixed with some creative thinking and a bit of hardware, can snap images like these that achieve the same results, though in lower quality.

The Raspberry Pi Foundation has also encouraged exploration with their device, which was the inspiration for the Astro Pi contest. The Astro Pi is a special Raspberry Pi which has been paired with the Sense HAT and sent to the International Space Station on a mission. A pair of these devices was sent with Python code written by school students and submitted to the Astro Pi competition. Thanks to Raspberry Pi, students had the chance to receive real outer space data to experiment with.

Chapter 3:

Raspbian Initial Set-up

Choose an Operating System

The first thing that one must do before beginning to set up their Raspberry Pi (RPI) is to choose their OS. This will determine how you will use your Raspberry Pi once configured, but it also means that you need to find an OS to mount to the MicroSD before you hook the computer together.

There are many options for OS's on the RPI website, with the most notable being Raspbian. They also include two ports of Ubuntu, Windows 10 IoT Core, OSMC, and LIBREELEC. There are many OS's outside of these options that will work for the small computer, but the best one to start with is its default: Raspbian.

Mike Thompson and Peter Green, known as mpthompson and plugwash, are the two primary benefactors of the Raspbian OS, which optimizes Debian for the RPI's ARMv6 CPU (now ARMv7 with the Pi 3). It is also very easy for beginners to handle, since it boots directly to the desktop, and packs a lot of software into an offline machine.

Available on the RPI software page is NOOBS. This makes it even easier for a new Raspberry Pi to install Raspbian and get the user into the machine. It provides a GUI that is easy to navigate and is very familiar to anyone who has become used to a Windows PC.

In this chapter, the reader will learn how to set up their Raspberry Pi 3, install Raspbian, tweak some initial configurations, and navigate the main menu to access all of the software that comes with the operating system.

NOOBS and Raspbian

For the simplest Raspberry Pi 3 set-up, you will only need a few necessary components to get started. An HDMI monitor, a (wireless) keyboard and mouse, a MicroUSB power supply, and a memory card loaded with an OS disc image are all that is needed to get started with the Raspberry Pi 3.

If you did not purchase a starter kit, you may not have an SD card loaded with the Raspbian image yet. Download the NOOBS .zip file hosted on the RPI website, extract its contents, and load them onto a newly-formatted microSD card.

Next, it is time to assemble your computer. The first step is to insert the memory card into its slot before putting any optional case on the machine. Next, plug in the monitor, keyboard, and mouse. Finally, attach the power supply before plugging it into the AC outlet.

Once the power supply is connected, the RPI will automatically power on and boot up. This is signaled by the "berry" images on the top of the screen, along with some system text. Then, you will be taken to the NOOBS set-up menu.

NOOBS will typically contain just one OS: Raspbian. Check the box next to this option, choose your language, and click Install. NOOBS will begin to install your OS onto your RPI3, which should take about forty-five minutes.

Initial Configuration

After the install is finished, the user will be brought to the bright desktop of Raspbian, complete with its great, big "berry" logo up front. Notice the Menu button and all of the icons on the screen. The first thing you will need to do is alter the Preferences in the Menu.

The Preferences option gives users easy access to their configurations without getting into messy command line operations. A new user should click "Expand Filesystem" so that they can resize the RPI partition and create more room to install new apps.

Finally, you may need to disable the Overscan setting so that your RPI3 will occupy the entire space in the monitor. If you do not see a thick black border around the screen activity, you will not need to do this.

The Desktop

Raspbian on RPI3 is the first Debian-based OS on the Raspberry Pi device to boot directly to the desktop GUI. Now that you have access to the desktop, you can begin to explore all of the software included in the OS.

Debian also has a huge collection of easily-downloadable software modules, which you can access to add games, tools, and functions to your machine.

Raspbian GUI

Before you even connect to the internet, explore the Raspbian GUI and become acquainted with the options made available to you. There is enough packed into the OS to make the RPI3 function like a general-purpose PC before you even have to download anything.

Like Windows PC's, the desktop of the Raspbian GUI comes with a taskbar, a Menu, and a Wastebasket. The taskbar will have some indicators and symbols on it, and the Menu will drop down a list of folders and programs.

Next to the Menu button are a few helpful shortcuts. First is the Epiphany Web Browser. Next to that are the File Explorer, the command line Terminal, Mathematica (an advanced calculation program), and Wolfram; a programming environment.

Directly across from these icons are some more items. You will see a Network Connections icon, which includes Wi-Fi services with RPI3. Next is the volume control, a CPU usage meter, a clock, and an eject symbol.

By opening the Menu, you will see a range of folders. The folders are: Programming, Office, Internet, Games, Accessories, Help, and Preferences. These are followed by Run and Shutdown.

The Programming folder contains programming tools and IDE's. You are welcomed to play with Scratch, Wolfram, Java, Sonic Pi, Node-RED, and Python, of course. Programmers of any level can pick up and experiment with these items.

The Office menu holds an entire office suite that is comparable to Microsoft Office. LibreOffice brings you Base, Calc, Draw, Impress, Math, and Writer, which enable the user to produce professional, high-quality work.

The Internet folder contains just a few things. Claws Mail is a Debian e-mail client. The Epiphany Web Browser is a lightweight web browser that comes as a default to Raspbian. Raspberry Pi Resources brings you to a helpful web page that gives educational info on Pi matters. The Magpi is a link to RPI news and buzz.

The Games menu will include only two options at first: Minecraft Pi and Python Games. Minecraft needs no introduction, but Minecraft Pi adds programming abilities to the player's control. Python Games are playable games made in Python that can be copied, modified, and hacked.

In the Accessories menu, the user will find a host of utilities that will allow them to control and configure their computer. These are included so that a beginning user will not have to download them on their own, including a PDF Viewer, Calculator, and SD Card Copier.

Selecting Help will reveal Debian Reference and Raspberry Pi Help. These options open web-links that bring the user official documentation on both topics.

The Preferences folder is very important and encloses some useful functions. These different settings allow the user to tweak and customize their audio device, keyboard, mouse, and main menu, along with other things.

Connect to the Internet

Unlike previous generations of Pi, the RPI3 comes with on-board WiFi capabilities. Instead of forcing users to purchase Wi-Fi adapters, it includes 802.11n Wireless LAN. Unfortunately, this can only receive 2.5 GHz signals.

To connect your RPI3 to a local Wi-Fi network, all that you will have to do is click the Network Connections icon on the taskbar. Like other Wi-Fi devices, it will display a list of nearby access points that the user can connect to. It's that easy.

If you are finding that you are unable to utilize the on-board WiFi, connect your RPI3 to the internet with an Ethernet cable. You will have to perform some Debian commands to update your system. Open the terminal and enter the following:

$ sudo apt-get update
$ sudo apt-get upgrade -y
$ sudo apt-get dist-upgrade -y
$ sudo rpi-update

A fully updated machine and some more commands are necessary to access the Bluetooth capabilities. Soon, these commands will be (partially) explained.

Install Software Packages

It is very easy to install new software and updates to your RPI once connected to the internet. By accessing Debian's software repository or the Raspberry Pi "app store," you can download new software with a few simple commands.

Debian uses a package handling tool known as the Advanced Package Tool (APT) to provide software to connected users. It is very easy to use and has two different faces: **apt-get/apt-cache** and **aptitude**.

The first option provides a quick, command-line approach to APT. If you know exactly what to download, it is faster to use **apt-get** than **aptitude**, though you will have to use **apt-cache** to find info on the package. **Aptitude** does what both commands do and brings it to the user in a rich, graphical layout.

For example: **aptitude install *xyz*** and **apt-get install *xyz*** will both install the **xyz** package to your system. Using **aptitude remove *xyz*** will have the same effect as **apt-get remove *xyz***, though **aptitude show *xyz*** is identical to **apt-cache show *xyz***, which will display information about **xyz**.

In addition, **aptitude** has a couple of unique functions. The **aptitude why *xyz*** and **aptitude why-not *xyz*** commands will explain why **xyz** should be installed, or what is keeping **xyz** from being installed, respectively.

Finally, The Pi Store is accessible through APT with the command, **sudo apt-get install pistore**. Then, to open The Pi Store, simply command **pistore** to the Terminal. This is how you open most programs in GNU/Linux.

Connect via Bluetooth

In order to access your Bluetooth capabilities, a few more initial commands must be made. After fully updating your OS with the above commands, enter the following:

$ sudo apt-get install bluez bluez-firmware blueman

This will install three packages: **bluez**, **bluez-firmware**, and **blueman**. After doing this, reboot your system.

Blueman puts the Bluetooth icon onto the taskbar of the Desktop GUI. By clicking the familiar icon, it will bring up a typical Bluetooth connection menu. Then, click "Devices..." to show the nearby Bluetooth devices and connect to them.

Bluetoothctl gives the user to configure their Bluetooth pairing and devices with the command line terminal. While using **bluetoothctl**, press **help** to reveal some useful info. Also, enter **power on**, **agent on**, and **scan on** to activate your Bluetooth, and **connect _MAC_** to pair the RPI3 to a device with the given MAC address.

Chapter 4:

Beginning Debian Administration

About Rasbian / Debian GNU

Raspbian is the name of the best Debian GNU/Linux port available for the Raspberry Pi 3. When it comes to GNU/Linux, Debian is one of the best distributions for the Raspberry Pi 3 because it is free and includes lots of free software. The latest stable release of Debian is called "Jessie", to follow the naming traditions that were started by its creator, Ian Murdock.

The Debian Manifesto was written by Ian Murdock during his time as a student at Purdue University in Lafayette, Indiana. His philosophy behind Debian matched the one set by the originators of GNU/Linux: users should own their computers and their software. Debian is popular because it is wholly free of charge to download and install and comes with APT, a repository of free software available to each user.

In just twenty years, Debian GNU/Linux has because the most popular free GNU/Linux distribution. It has grown a vast population of users that work together to build and grow Debian with their computing prowess. The community behind

Debian has inspired the Raspberry Pi Foundation to endorse Raspbian as their primary operating system.

In this chapter, a beginning Raspberry Pi user can find an understanding of Debian terms and commands. They will figure out how to move around a Linux computer with the command line terminal, and how to start managing their files and user permissions. Finally, the user can learn to take control of their computer processes through the command line and remotely via secure shell (SSH).

The Terminal and Commands

Raspbian provides a lush GUI that guides users to their favorite programs quickly and easily, but the direct way to influence your Raspberry Pi 3 is through the terminal. You can find a link to the terminal through the taskbar. The command line terminal controls a "shell," which is the interpreter through which a user inputs commands and reads returned information. There are different types of shells. "Dash" is the Debian Almquist shell. GNU/Linux users often use "bash," or Bourne Again shell, which came from the original Bourne shell, called "sh."

To speak to the computer through the shell, a user must use commands. Commands are usually strings of text which are read as a set of directions by the computer. Most commands are like sentences, and the "words" in the sentence are programs, options, signals, arguments, paths, etc. The command that a user would use to acquire a software package using APT looks like this:

pi@raspberrypi: ~ $ sudo apt-get *package_name*

The prefix to the command in the example identifies the user's name, the name of their computer, their home path, and their permission level. On the other side of the colon, the user inputs the command.

In the prefix, **pi** is the username, and **raspberrypi** is the name of the computer. "~" stands for the home path, which would be revealed to a user logged in as **root**. To log in as **root**, enter the command, **sudo su**. This forces the command, **su**, which switches user to **root** after the entry of a password.

Once the user is logged in as **root**, the "$" will change into a "#" which indicates administrative permission. Using the command, **sudo**, executes the following commands with temporary **root** permission. When using administrative power, a user must be careful to ensure that they understand their commands so that they are less likely to force harmful executions within their system.

In addition, the owner of a Debian system may not want to grant total access to each user. In order to prevent mistakes and user tampering through networks, a Raspbian user must understand basic GNU/Linux administration.

Basic Administration

Raspbian, like other GNU/Linux operating systems, are multi-user and multi-session. Up to five users may contact and command a computer that is running Debian GNU/Linux by accessing it through a network. A user without a login account may not connect through their own computers.

When you first set up Raspbian, you will be prompted to enter a password for the **root** account. From that point forward, users will be asked for a username and password when booting or accessing that computer. Multiple accounts can be created later. Files and directories have individual permission settings that are attributed to the different users in a system.

A user that is logged into the system as **root** has the ability to change settings, and has total control over the movement and deletion of files and directories. **Root** may be known as the "super-user" account because of its power. It can create files and set the permissions for each lesser user on the account. The super-user can also modify configuration files with text editors.

When logged into an active session in the terminal, one can switch between the multiple sessions with Alt and the F-keys. By pressing Alt+F2, a second terminal will open, and it will prompt a username and password. The same thing will happen when using Alt in combination with F3-F5. A user may switch between a **root** account and a lesser account to test their permission settings.

By using the command, **sudo**, a user can temporarily invoke **root** privileges without needing to log out and back into the system. Only users who are given permission to use this command may borrow its power. Also, the program logs every instance that a user commands **sudo**. A user may also command **sudo -i** to log into the **root** account through the shell.

If you need a reminder that will tell you if you currently have **root** control, you may enter the command, **whoami** to find out. You do not always want to use that power when modifying files; sometimes it is good to be reminded by the computer that an action is dangerous. You may also use command **groups** to see which groups your current account is in. Commanding **su** allows you to switch user accounts.

When you want to list the permission settings for a certain file or directory, use the command **ls -l** and the path of the file. Inputting the command **ls -l /home/writ.txt** may return the following information:

-rwxr-xr-- 1 daniel games 118 Dec 30 2015 /home/writ.txt

The mode is the string of hyphens and letters at the beginning of this return. There are ten characters in the string. The first character indicates whether the target is a directory or a file. A file is designated by a '-' while a 'd' would indicate that it is a directory.

The remaining nine characters in the string are grouped into triplets. The first triplet of characters represents the user's permissions with the file. The second triplet stands for the permissions within the group, and the final triplet shows the permissions for other users.

In this example, "rwx" shows that the user, **daniel**, may read, write, and execute the file. Next, the "r-x" explains that users within the **games** group may only read or execute it. Finally, other users outside of the group may only read, not execute or write the file.

One may adjust the permission settings for a particular file by using the command **chmod**. This command has the ability to add, subtract, or set permissions within the user, group, and others triplets. Some **chmod** commands may look like this:

$ chmod u+r *reptile* (This adds read to the *reptile* permissions granted to the user.)

$ chmod g-x *reptile* (This revokes execution permissions for *reptile* within the group.)

$ chmod o-rw *reptile* (This command revokes reading and writing privileges from non-group users.)

$ chmod a=rwx *reptile* (In this command, **a** means all. This command sets all user permissions to read, write, and execute.)

File Structure and Handling Archives

The way that Raspbian structures its files and directories (folders to Windows users) is a little different than what most desktop users are accustomed to. A file path in Windows uses back-slashes (\) to separate the items; GNU/Linux systems, including Raspbian, use forward-slashes (/). A Windows directory may also start with C:\, D;\, E:\, etc. Linux file systems are all arranged beneath **root**, the master directory.

Known as "/", **root** is the base of the tree; all other directories branch from the ultimate directory. The files and directories beneath "/" can be arranged in any way by the owner of the system, but there is a standard. Typically, the directory structure of GNU/Linux systems are matched to the "Filesystem Hierarchy Structure" (FHS), defined by the Free Standards Group.

Files that are vital to the booting process of your Raspberry Pi will be held in directories including **/boot, /bin**, and **/sys**. The **/dev** directory would contain drivers and other important system files. The **/etc** directory holds network and other configuration files, and the **/usr** directory contains even more directories, sub-directories that have their own organized hierarchy, and organize non-critical binary files and data.

The directory that concerns the user the most is their **/home** directory, which holds all of their personal files and settings. The majority of the user's software and personal configurations are put in this directory. The home directory of the user **root** is found at **/root**, not to be confused with **/**.

As soon as the user begins a session in the command line terminal, they will start in their home directory. They will be presented with a blank command line prompt instead of a visual display of folders and items. A user may input **pwd** (print working directory) to be given their current path. Using **cd** and then giving a path will navigate the user to that location in their computer. If you enter **cd** alone, you will be taken to your home directory.

Once inside of a directory, a user can use the **ls** command to display the contents within the directory. A list of files and directories within the current working directory will be displayed, like so:

$ cd
$ pwd
/home/daniel
$ ls
Games Music Work

There are shortcuts that you may use in Debian to prevent yourself from having to enter a full directory path to navigate. "**.**" is your current working directory, and "**..**" represents the parent directory to your current working directly.

```
$ cd
$ pwd
/home/daniel
$ cd Games
$ ls
Game1 Game1.txt
$ cd .
$ pwd
/home/daniel/Games
$ cd ..
$ pwd
/home/daniel/
```

Moving, creating, and deleting the directories and files in your system is also carried out with simple commands. By commanding **mkdir *dirname***, the user can make a new directory within their current working directory. To move it, they would use **mv *dirname newdir*,** and to remove a directory, they would command **rmdir *dirname***. If *newdir* does not already exist at the time that the **mv** command targets it, that directory will be created.

```
$ pwd
/home/daniel/Work
$ ls
Aa Bb
$ mv Aa Cc
$ ls
Bb Cc
$ cd Cc
$ ls
Aa
```

When you need to read some helpful information about an item in your system, use the **man** command. The pages that are returned are called manual pages, or "manpages" for short. By inputting **man *quest***, the contents of the **quest** program's manual page will be displayed through a pager, usually the pager program known as **less**. To display a certain page within the manual document, you would enter a number before the keyword, like **man 2 *quest*** to display page 2.

Various text editors exist within Raspbian that one can use to write and modify text files. **Nano** is a popular text editor that creates, rewrites, and reads text files. You can also create text files by using the command **echo**, which is used to display text in shell scripts, and a redirection. For example, the command **echo "newtxt" > *newo*** would create a file named **newo** that contained the text "newtxt". You may also add to the end of the text file with a double-redirect: **echo "newtxt2" >> *newo***.

When searching for certain files and directories within your Raspbian system, use the **find** and **grep** commands. **Find** is used to search through your data structure by a filename: **find *dir* -name *filename*. Grep** is used when you only know some of the content of your search target. Commanding **grep *keyword*** will return lines that match that keyword.

Like when returning manual pages, a pager is used when expecting a return that is too long to fit on the screen. **More** is the original pager, and one may command **more *gamefile.txt*** to pass the target through the pager, displaying it one page at a time, advanced by a tap of the spacebar. **Less** does even more, so it is more often used than the original pager.

Chapter 4: Beginning Debian Administration

When it is time to download more software to your Raspbian system, one should take advantage of the Advanced Packaging Tool to get their free software. **Apt-get** downloads secure, hosted software so that users do not have to search the internet and unpack them into their system manually. If you do want to download software that is not available through APT, you must learn to "unzip" compressed archives known as "tarballs".

First, a user will need to install **gzip** through their command line terminal. This is done by commanding # **apt-get install gzip**. In this example, the user is logged in as **root** as has a # in front of their command, indicating **sudo** power.

After it is installed, you may use the command **gunzip** to open and extract .gz archives that you have downloaded. It may be named something like **puzzlebox.tar.gz**, so you would command **gunzip puzzlebox.tar.gz** to extract **puzzlebox.tar** into the current working directory.

This .tar archives is known as a "tarball". It is a cluster of files bound together by the **tar** program that will be compressed by **gzip** to make an archive. It keeps the same directory structure if subdirectories are involved. To extract the files from within, command **tar -xvf puzzlebox.tar**.

The latest update of **tar** has added the option to extract .tar.gz or .tgz files without having to run them through **gzip** first. To do this, command **tar -zxvf puzzlebox.tar.gz**.

If you want to compress your own source archives for internet distribution, you may use both of these utilities. To make a .tgz archive, you must first use **tar** to create a tarball. To compress your file or files into a tarball, use this command: # **tar -cvf** *zip.tar zipfile01 zipfile02*. Both "zipfiles" will be compressed into zip.tar.

Then, use **gzip** to compress your new tarball into a .tgz archive. The following command will execute this process: # **gzip zip.tar**. This will produce a new archive, zip.tgz.

Managing Processes

If you have ever needed to remedy a frozen Windows computer, you may be familiar with the task manager, a window that helps the user pick and end unruly processes. In Raspbian GNU/Linux, a user must figure out how to find processes and control them manually.

Every process that is executed by the computer bears a Process ID (PID). The first process from the moment a computer boots is known as **init,** and this has a PID of 1. To find other PID's, use the command **ps**. This command can return several different batches of processes. **Ps** lists the current processes and PIDs, and **ps -A** shows all processes and their PIDs. If you already know the name of a process, command **pidof** *process* will return the PID of the given process.

By passing your **ps** return through **grep** with the pipe character, "|", you can search through the list of processes. For example, **ps aux | grep** *unknown* will return a list of processes with "unknown" in the name. This is useful because you never want to forcefully terminate the wrong processes, especially if you do not know what they do.

When you are sure about terminating a process, use the **kill**, **pkill**, and **killall** commands. The safest way to end a process is by commanding **kill -15 *PID***. The signal, **-15**, tells **kill to** safely end the process. The same effect is reached with -

TERM. The signal, **-9**, is used to harshly kill a process, ending it immediately. **-KILL** is used the same way. Take care when forcing processes to end with **sudo**. To end multiple processes at once, you may do them with just one command, like so: **kill -15 425 584 593**.

Pkill can be used to kill a command if you only know its name and not its PID. Use **pgrep** before taking this step to accurately search for the right process. **Killall** also uses a given process name to kill all instances of the named process as well as any processes that it has created.

Chapter 5:

A Primer to Python 3

Python is regarded as the most fitting programming language for the Raspberry Pi. It is a free, open-source language, and it is optimized for beginning coders to learn easily.

It has a huge library of free modules that can be imported with a simple command. Instead of having to code their own utilities, Python can import modules like **os** and **random** to bring in functions that will be useful when writing new programs.

You can find the Python 3 Integrated Development and Learning Environment (IDLE) in the drop-down Menu of Raspbian's desktop. There are two ways to control Python 3: through the interactive shell or through an IDE such as IDLE. The IDLE is better for handling big tasks like writing programs and defining functions.

The IDLE makes it very easy for one to write in Python and learn while they are doing it. The text field is formatted to display the code clearly and easily. The text will change colors when the user inputs code and the interpreter distinguishes what the user is doing, displaying tooltips and other helpful hints.

Working within the IDLE will help the user write programs easily and quickly, which will help automate tasks when creating projects with the Raspberry Pi 3. Support for Raspberry Pi functions such as the GPIO pins are available for import as modules within Python.

Python is known as an object-oriented programming language. Python makes it very easy to create classes and objects. An object is a unique instance of a data structure, defined by its class. A class is a prototype for an object that contains definitions for a set of attributes that characterize any class object.

Within classes, you can define functions which are known as methods. When calling a method from an object, it can perform as a function and takes an argument. Also, Python supports class inheritance, which means that classes that are derived from an original class receive the characteristics of that class.

Object-oriented programming is not unique to Python, but Python offers the power of object-oriented programming to beginners by simplifying many of the processes involved. It is easy to create, modify, and understand objects and classes, and then utilize them in your own programs.

In addition to being easy to write, Python also handles some things behind the scenes that a beginner may not want to be concerned with. Python allocates its memory automatically, it does not require the user to declare data types, and it is easier to read and write files than it is in other similar programming languages. Python 3 is the best programming language for a beginning Raspberry Pi 3 user.

Why Python 3?

Raspbian offers its users access to both the Python 2 and Python 3 IDLE's, although Python 3 is the better choice for users who are beginning to learn to program in Python. There are a few minor differences that make Python 3 a better programming language. It is up to the user to choose, because there are a few reasons why one may need to stick with Python 2, though a new user may not be concerned with those details.

Python 3 was built and released by its creator as the definitive step forward in the line of Python programming languages, and is not backwards-compatible. Python 2 has limited support because it is the old language, and Python 3 has become the new standard; but one can still use Python 2 successfully.

Some software that was developed with Python 2 and is intended for use with other Python 2 software has not yet been ported to Python 3. A port is when a user takes a program and edits or re-writes the code to be compatible with a different system. Most new software will be written for Python 3, and Python 3 will be built to adapt to new software changes, but Python 2 may still be the best choice for some projects.

Another big change that makes a difference between Python 2 and Python 3 is that, by default, Python 3 code is encoded with Unicode, UTF-8. Python 2 is encoded in ASCII and does not support the wider range of characters available for Python 3. Unicode is becoming the universal text encoder used internationally, so Python 3 is once again better suited for future applications.

There are other, finer changes that have taken place during the move from Python 2 to Python 3. These changes are more important to advanced users with a lot of experience with Python as well as other object-oriented programming languages. A new user will not notice these details while learning Python 3.

Python 3 was built with the new user in mind, and it is a language that wants to help beginning learners grasp object-oriented programming before they delve into the intricate code behind the scenes. Because of this reason, it is easier for a new learner to focus their energy on studying the newest rules, rather than concerning themselves too much on how the tiny changes will affect their projects.

Get To Know Python

In Python, just about everything is an "object". An object stands for a piece of data, a snippet of code, or a whole library of functions. Classes are objects. Modules are objects. Functions too, are objects. Objects can be passed as arguments and they can be called like methods. An object is named by the variable that stands for it, which needs to start with a letter, and is typically a word or phrase and is case-sensitive.

A variable is the name that one gives to a type of data, a function, a class, or another object that the user wants to utilize. One can think of a variable as a bucket that keeps its contents within, like a container that can be opened when one needs the data inside. A variable, in reality, is a numbered reference to the piece of data, which lives within the code.

There are three data types that are used within Python 3: strings, integers, and floating-point numbers. A string, simply put, is a word or series of characters. An integer is a whole number, positive or negative, or zero. A decimal or a fraction cannot be an integer; they are, instead, known as floating-point numbers. The different data types take up differing amounts of space, so one should know not to overuse unnecessary floating-point numbers.

When deciding which data type to use in a given variable, the user does not have to explicitly command Python 3 to read it as such. For example:

```
>>> term = 'final'  # This is a comment
>>> print(term)  # Comments are not read nor executed by
Python 3
final
>>> type(term)  # Comments help explain code to reading
users
(class 'str')
```

As seen above, it is very simple to assign data to a variable; you just use the = character, and Python recognizes the given data as a string. Passing an object through the **type()** function will return the object's class. You can also use this function to determine what type of data will be returned from a given function.

When you need your code to do something for you, you will need to use a function. A function is an object that takes an argument into its parentheses and returns a value after performing its own programmed code. Some functions such as **print()**, **type()**, and **len()** are part of Python 3 by default.

Other functions are defined by the user to work within a greater document of code.

A function may be defined in the interactive shell like so:

```
>>> def print2(x):  # This is a def statement that defines print2()
...        print(x)  # print2() will print the given argument once
...        print(x)  # Then it will print it again on the next line
...        # Hit Enter or Return on an empty prompt to finish defining
>>> print2('obj')  # using function print2()
obj
obj
```

Blocks of code are delimited by indentations in the code or "whitespaces", which visually group together correlated lines of code. In other programming languages, it is generally good coding practice to visually group together the lines of code that work together such as in a loop. In Python 3, you must indent lines of code so that they may work together in that group.

When a block of code is read, the Python parser starts at the very top, then it moves down reading line after line. It carries out each line of code and moves on, never to go back and perform that line of code again before the program ends. Unless directed by flow control actions such as loops, a user will have to write the same lines over and over again to achieve repeated executions.

A 'While Loop' is a method of flow control that is condition-controlled. What that means is that the contents of a While Loop will repeat in order eternally while the condition is True. The condition must become False to end the infinite loop. True and False are Boolean values, which are important to flow control.

Another type of flow control is the 'For Loop', which is collection-controlled. A loop that is controlled by a collection means that it will repeat for each iteration in a series. Instead of being controlled and ended by a Boolean value, it will repeat once for each iteration and then move onto the rest of the code.

When composing function definitions, it is easier to compose a Python file (.py) with your IDLE, and test-run the program from within the environment. Attempting to define a function in the interactive shell is a much more tedious venture. The following example is formatted to be entered into an IDE, not the shell:

Write - whileDemo.py:

```
1| def print3(x): # Defining a new function, print()
2|    var = 3  # x will print this many times
3|    while var > 0: # while var is greater than 0
4|        print(x)  # print the given data
5|        var -= 1  # the data in var is reduced by 1
6| print3('three')  # the function will use the string, 'three'
```

Run - whileDemo.py:

three
three
three

This is an example of a program that uses a while loop to print given data until a condition becomes False. While **var** is greater than zero, it does two things in order: first, it prints the given, x, then it reduces **var** by 1. After completing the block of code, it checks to see if **var** is still greater than 0. If it is, it repeats the process. After the third time, **var** is reduced to 0, and the program no longer repeats that doublet of code.

Notice the structure of the lines of code within the two statements. The **print3()** function creates a variable, **var**, then defines a While Loop statement. You can clearly distinguish the contents of the function definition from the contents of the loop definition. This syntax is mandatory in Python 3.

Write - forDemo.py:

```
1| def print4(x):  # define new function
2|     for i in range(0, 4):  # for each item in this range
3|         print(x)  # prints given variable
4| print(list(range(0, 4))) #there are four items in this list
5| print4('four') #prints once for each item
```

Run - forDemo.py:

```
[0, 1, 2, 3]
four
four
four
four
```

The above program, **forDemo.py**, does three things: it defines a function **print4()**, prints the list **range(0, 4)**, and carries out the function. The reason that is prints the list is so that you can see that there are four items in the list **range(0, 4)**, which this For Loop uses to iterate its repetitions.

The **range(x, y)** function returns a list of integers by using the two given parameters. Parameter **x** stands for the first integer in the list, and parameter **y** stands for the place where the list will end. Because 4 is used for **y**, 4 is not in the list because the list ends at **y**.

More Flow Control Techniques

Sometimes, a program must respond to non-binary conditions, meaning that there are more interactive possibilities than the return of a True or False value. Especially when your program expects user input, it should be ready to anticipate varying data and respond accordingly without crashing.

'If' statements and 'Else' statements are used in conjunction to account for situations in which the condition of the loop depends on a different number of possibilities. For example, when prompted for input, a user can enter anything, but a program may only need one type of data. So, **if** a user inputs a string, one thing will happen. **Else**, the program will carry out a different function.

If and Else statements work together to lead the user through different programs depending on their input. "Elif" statements are used to add even more paths to the flow of your program. These conditional statements can be used to take the user through different program experiences depending on their input, giving the user greater control over what the program will do for them. A program cannot anticipate input; it can only react depending on the programmer's pre-determined paths of flow.

In some cases, a loop may need to "reset", going back to the first line of the code so that it can perform the block of code once again. This is performed by a 'Continue' statement, which is a method of flow control that is used within loops. Continue statements are there to handle situations in which a user enters the incorrect input and needs to be led through the program again.

When the flow of a program need to be halted dead in its tracks, a 'Break' statement is necessary. While working within a system of "If"s and "Else"s, a Break statement may be used so that the user has the option to end a loop and exit the flow of a program. This is useful for when the user needs to quit their application and wants the program to end itself safely.

If you have ever tried to perform a function in Python but entered an incorrect command, you would have noticed an 'Exception', which serves to alert the user that they have done something wrong. These Exceptions have different types and are meant to help a programmer find the mistakes in their code. Users that input incorrect data can also raise an Exception, which can be predicted by the programmer.

Exception Handling is the technique of anticipating Exceptions during program execution, and writing code that will react accordingly. Programmers can define and raise their own Exceptions within their programs. By doing this, a programmer can create efficient and diverse flow paths within their program, creating an intuitive and rich experience for the intended user.

Data Structures of Python 3

In Python 3, it becomes easy to maximize the efficiency of your code when you start to master data organization and structure. Creating and handling different sequences allows you to manage your variables. By indexing, slicing, and otherwise accessing your data sequences, you can take a lot of information out of the same data.

When printing words and letters, a user creates a string, but a string is more than just a word. A string is a sequence of characters that can be indexed and sliced, but a string is unable to be changed, making it immutable.

Lists are contained between square brackets ([]) and contain different pieces of data, separated by commas. Lists are mutable sequences, meaning that the sequence of data can be modified and trimmed once it is in a list.

```
>>> list1 = ['1', 1, 1.0]  # this list holds a str, int, and float
>>> list1[0]  # the first item, a string, is at index 0
'1'
>>> list1[1]  # integer 1 is kept at index 1
1
>>> list1[2]  # the final item is a floating-point number, 1.0
1.0
>>> list1[0:2] #this is called a slice
['1', 1]
>>> list2 = ['2']  # creating a second list
>>> list1 = list1 + list2  # concatenate two lists
>>> list1  # list1 has been changed
['1', 1, 1.0, '2']
```

Tuples are immutable sequences that are used to group items that are meant to stay together. Those sequences are held together by parentheses, and their contents are separated by commas. They can contain different types of data like lists, but their contents cannot be modified after creation.

```
>>> hotTuple = (6, 6.0, '6')  # create one tuple
>>> coldTuple = (9, 9.0, '9')  # create a second tuple
>>> hotTuple = coldTuple + hotTuple  # can be concatenated
>>> hotTuple  # display new hotTuple
(9, 9.0, '9', 6, 6.0, '6')
>>> len(hotTuple)  # return integer equal to number of items
6
>>> hotTuple[0] = 90  # futile attempt to change a tuple item
Traceback (most recent call last):
  File "<stdin>", line 1, in <module>
TypeError: 'tuple' object does not support item assignment
```

Dictionaries in Python 3 are like lists of lists, known in other programming languages as "associative arrays". Dictionaries, kept in curly brackets ({}), list key-value pairs, which can be handily indexed when in need of a list of keys, values, or both.

```
>>> pure = {'good': 123, 'evil': 321}  # make a new dict.
>>> pure['neutral'] = 0  # create a new key, assign a value
>>> pure  # display pure dictionary
('good': 123, 'evil': 321, 'neutral': 0}
>>> pure.keys()  # display the keys in pure dictionary
['good', 'evil', 'neutral']
>>> pure.values()  # display the values in pure dictionary
[123, 321, 0]
>>> pure['good']  # display the value assigned to good key
```

Higher Structures

Sometimes, a Python user will utilize functions that contain a period, such as **listNew.append('10')**, which would add string '10' to a list. These are functions called methods that are defined within objects known as modules. A module is a type of class, which are very important when building Python programs of increasingly complex depth.

You may need to generate a random number in your program, but Python does not start with this ability; you must import a module. To enable random number generation, use an **import** command, like in this example:

>>> **import random** # this imports the random module
>>> **random.randint(1, 6)** # the two arguments determine the range
4

The method, **randint()**, is contained within **random**, which is a class of functions. In this case, **random** is a module. Not all classes are modules. Many methods already exist in Python 3, like **.append()**, but you can define your own classes and methods within your program.

```
class Human:  # this defines a class. they should begin with
uppercase
    def me_method(self):  # within a class, define methods
        print "I am a Human"  # this is what the method does.
c = Human()  # referencing the class with a variable object
c.me_method()  # perform a method that belongs to a class
```

Chapter 6:

Raspberry Pi Systems

With the Raspberry Pi 3, users have discovered a world of computing tools and education within the tiny computer and its free software. By embarking on a learning journey of Debian systems and Python 3 programming, a new user will have a long road ahead of them that will teach them new ideas and show them how to truly take control of computers.

The other side of the coin is that the Raspberry Pi 3 can influence not only an internal system, but systems that exist in the physical realm, as well. The Raspberry Pi 3 has the capability to be the brain of many exciting applications, including gaming, entertainment, and tinkering. With some ingenious creativity and the dedication to learning and practicing, an experienced Pi user can create machines that can automate and protect their home. This chapter contains a few examples.

RetroPie Emulator Cabinet

The Raspberry Pi 3 boasts an impressive processor for its size, and it will not stress your machine to turn it into a full-time retro gaming station. Thanks to an easily-installed operating system called RetroPie, the Pi 3 can be set up to emulate retro gaming systems which will work with your keyboard or other USB peripherals.

You do not need much more than the basics for this project: a Raspberry Pi 3, a monitor, a keyboard, a mouse, and a microSD card. The sky is the limit with this project, however. You can build your RetroPie computer into anything from a Raspberry Pi-powered gaming console with handheld controllers, to a fully decked-out arcade-style machine loaded with four joysticks and a bunch of colorful buttons.

RetroPie 4.0 was announced to be released on the RetroPie website during August of 2016. The latest OS image can be found and downloaded from the site. After unzipping the .img file, you will need to install it as a disk image onto your MicroSD card.

Depending on your PC operating system, you will need to use a different program to mount the disk image onto the MicroSD card. Of course, the card will need to be formatted, but once the RetroPie OS is installed onto the memory card, it is ready to be placed into the Pi.

Before connecting your Raspberry Pi with RetroPie, connect the device that you want to use to control the games because the OS will configure the controls upon its first boot at the Welcome screen. You can also configure additional controllers through the main menu of EmulationStation.

Once you are able to move around the menu, you will want to connect your Pi to Wi-Fi. This is done in the RetroPie menu, found in EmulationStation. You can load any game ROMs into the system through a Wi-Fi network, Ethernet, or USB stick.

To transfer ROMs into the system with a USB stick, make sure that the flash drive is formatted to FAT32 or NTFS, and create a folder called **retropie**. Plug the USB drive into the Pi, wait for it to finish blinking, then plug the flash drive back into your computer to put tracks into **retropie/roms**. Once the ROMs are loaded, plug the stick into the Raspberry Pi and then restart the computer. To transfer ROMs through a network, it will need to be wired through Ethernet or connected through SSH File Transfer Protocol (SFTP).

The games, once installed, can be configured to work with your keyboard, USB gaming controllers, and even real arcade parts. USB gaming controllers and controller adaptors can be found online in many different models and layouts. Just configure them through the RetroPie menu.

To use real arcade parts, however, requires another piece: The I-PAC keyboard encoder. This piece of hardware by Ultimarc can convert input signals from classic, wired arcade joysticks and buttons into a Pi-compatible signal through full-speed USB 2.0.

The Raspberry Pi 3 is the best system for running RetroPie OS's because of its faster processor. You may still encounter speed issues during games, and they may play faster or slower than their true console versions. Unfortunately, due to the nature of emulation, some games will never play at their original speed on the Raspberry Pi 3, but there are some options that can be set to improve performance.

The configuration file for RetroArch emulators is at **/opt/retropie/configs/all/retroarch.cfg**. When editing this file, you can change **video_smooth = false** and **rewind_enable = false** to deactivate some fluffy features that you will not need. In addition, a user can overclock their

Raspberry Pi's processor to force faster processing speeds. This can be found through **sudo raspi-config** and is best done with an aluminum heatsink attached to the Raspberry Pi.

Raspberry Pi Home Theater

As small as it is, the Raspberry Pi 3 is a qualified home theater machine with the ability to handle your large-scale media files and play them with peak performance. Kodi is a free, open-source media player with the ability to send media data across a local network and bring you web services such as Spotify and YouTube. In addition, it can access TV shows, movies, music, and DVDs through one user-friendly interface.

Just like a RetroPie system, it does not require more than the basics for this project; you will mount a different OS onto the MicroSD card, LibreELEC in this case. An HDMI cable is recommended for displaying high-definition media on a suitable television, and a Bluetooth remote control or infrared remote control adaptor are optional extras. Also, you may wish to use a USB sound card to improve sound quality.

LibreELEC is known as "Just enough OS for Kodi," and is also free and open-source. This is a very easy OS to install and configure for the Raspberry Pi, and it is hosted on the Raspberry Pi download site. Because of its ease of install and its light-weight form, it is the quickest and simplest way to turn your Pi into a dedicated Kodi machine.

Installation is as easy as downloading the "LibreELEC USB-SD Creator" app from their website, https://libreelec.tv/downloads/. Once downloaded, simply plug in the drive that you wish to format and install LibreELEC onto, and let the wizard guide you through the simple process. Once finished, your MicroSD card is ready to be mounted into the Raspberry Pi 3 and booted.

To access LibreELEC without interrupting the Kodi experience, you can set up a Secure Shell (SSH) by using a program such as Putty to send remote commands. By default, the SSH login is user: **root**, password: **libreelec**. You may also use Samba. Samba is a tool that allows Linux / Unix computers to transfer files to and from Windows computers on the same network. This is known as SMB/CIFS.

The way that Kodi is able to host so many videos, pictures, and other media is through Media Sources. When you enter any of the media folders or the Filemanager, you will see that you can "Add Sources," which would be a drive or directory on your LibreELEC device. The place where you will physically store those media files is up to you, but your Raspberry Pi will not be able to hold much in its own memory.

There are three ways to connect Kodi to your media: adding internal Media Sources, network file sharing, and internet streaming. For smaller items such as Pictures, you may just want to add a Media Source that links to the directory on your Raspberry Pi which holds your pictures. You may also use SFTP so that you can access shared files and folders hosted online.

To access internet streams as though they were files in your Media Sources, you may use a custom .strm file or a standard playlist (.pls or .m3u). To create a .strm file, simply create a text-file with the extension .strm and edit it to contain the direct URL-link to the stream. If you are creating a list of playlists, save the .strm and .pls files into a directory and link to that directory as a Media Source. To add .strm files to the library with cover art and summaries, you can use an NFO file like any other video file.

One thing to note is that a user running LibreELEC on their Raspberry Pi may notice some performance crawling and the colorful rainbow square icon. These are issues caused by inefficient power usage. To solve this problem, use a 5V, 2.5A power supply so that you can supply the Pi with an adequate amount of power.

Play With Electronics

There are many computing applications that can be tackled by the Raspberry Pi, but some of the most engaging projects that involve the Pi are electronic and function within the real world. Because of the processing that it promises for a low price and its 40 GPIO pins, the Raspberry Pi 3 is a popular and capable choice for electronic tinkerers.

Beginning learners of electronics will find a lot of fun in a kit that contains a breadboard, jumper cables, and a whole bunch of electronic components. Many popular Raspberry Pi starter kits include necessary pieces such as resistors, capacitors, and switches.

Those who are interested in building circuits must first understand Ohm's Law, which describes the relationship between voltage (V), resistance (R), and current (I).

$V = IR$, or $I = V/R$

In summary, the voltage supplied to a circuit must be equal to the current multiplied by the resistance. A student can use the principle of Ohm's Law to build safe, complete circuits in which the right amount of power is distributed to their components.

When planning and building circuits, a breadboard is an indispensable tool. A breadboard is a grid of contacts into which electrical components can be plugged, connecting them all into a solder-less circuit. The Raspberry Pi would be connected into the breadboard by GPIO pins, activated and controlled through Python or another programming language.

An even easier way to delve into electronic manipulation is by purchasing a Pibrella, made by Cyntech. This is a Hardware Attached on Top (HAT) board that packs a lot of fun components into one neat system that stacks neatly atop the Raspberry Pi 3. With the Pibrella, you can learn to control LED's, simple speakers, and GPIO pins without fussing with wires and resistors.

In the earlier days of the Raspberry Pi, it was not as easy to control the GPIO pins and manipulate hardware through Python. Now, however, it's as easy as pie! Python library modules have been developed by influential users that make it simple for new users to program code that will affect the real world through electronic circuits. Just import **RPi.GPIO** within your Python 3 code.

If you are using a Pibrella, this handy device also comes with a proprietary Python library. This is done through the following terminal commands:

apt-get update
apt-get upgrade
apt-get install python-pip
pip install pibrella

This example updates APT's libraries and the software. Then, it installs Pip; Python's own packaging tool. Finally, the packaging tool is used to install the Pibrella Python Libraries. Afterwards, you can import **pibrella** within your Python 3 code to access the methods that control the colorful pieces of the Pibrella board.

It is unlikely that you will encounter a hazard when working with the Pibrella, but tinkerers who wish to deal with more complex and powerful electronics need to learn, first, about the right safety precautions. One should not handle high-voltage components until they are totally prepared.

Any circuit that draws power from a home AC outlet has lethal power. In general, do not work on any active circuit; unplug first. Keep your work area bone-dry and free of clutter to prevent accidents and flare-ups. If you wish to use a soldering iron, take utmost precaution and always wear safety goggles. Finally, always work in a well-ventilated space and keep a fire extinguisher, first-aid kit, and a telephone nearby.

Light Up Your Pi

A great way to dazzle your friends with your Raspberry Pi skills is by lighting up an LED matrix with bright colors and composite imagery. Fortunately for you, it does not take a mastermind to play with LED's; many Python libraries exist that are compatible with different hardware.

Because bigger LED matrices are more complicated and draw much more power, it is wise to start with a small, 8x8 LED matrix. It is possible to build your own LED matrix, but some have already been developed for the Raspberry Pi. They connect to the Pi's GPIO pins and can sit on top of the board like a HAT, or can be connected by a ribbon wire. Some, like the Pi MATRIX available at www.mypishop.com are kits to be assembled at home.

Also available for purchase is the official Raspberry Pi Sense HAT, which is a fun LED matrix and more. The HAT that plugs directly into the Pi's GPIO pins includes an 8x8 LED matrix as well as a gyroscope, accelerometer, and other fun capabilities. This HAT is also supported by its own Python library with lots of helpful methods to make it easy to program the HAT through Python.

This is how you install the Sense HAT software:

sudo apt-get update
sudo apt-get install sense-hat
sudo reboot

From within Python, you can use different methods to manipulate the LED matrix, including drawing pixel by pixel, entering a string to be interpreted and displayed, and rotation options.

One thing to be aware of is that bigger LED matrices require a lot of power handling, a lot more than what the Raspberry Pi was built for. Even worse, a circuit with an LED matrix experiences many current spikes as lights flicker on and off with varying amounts of power. For systems like these, a strong power supply, such as the ones used for PC's, might be necessary.

As the LED matrix works, the display requires constant updates as each LED is sent signals hundreds of times in a second. To operate an LED matrix may use up to 30% of the

CPU power of a Raspberry Pi 3, so you may be unable to run many operations at the same time as an active matrix.

After learning how to operate an LED matrix through Python, one can begin to learn how to build real-world applications that utilize GPIO pins and headers. This is the domain of embedded systems, in which a computer controls multiple things, including LED's, LCD's, speakers, and other electronics.

Python-Enabled Web Server

By enabling your Raspberry Pi 3 to act as a dedicated web server, your machine can host a web page through which you can access your content. In this way, a Raspberry Pi can be programmed to host images and other media on your home web page. Through a bit of quick programming and some camera configuration, you can use your Raspberry Pi to set up a surveillance system that will alert you of intruders.

The RPI is perfectly suited to act as a web server with Apache. To use a typical home PC to host a web server is possible, although it would tax the resources on the system, making for a slow computer and an unstable web server. Because of the Pi's low price, you can purchase the inexpensive computer to be a dedicated web server.

Apache, a free and open-source program, can help you get your Pi web page online quickly. 60% of all websites use Apache to host their content. It supports HTML as well as PHP, giving web developers the tools needed to host dynamic web content.

To install **apache2**, use the command **sudo apt-get install apache —y**. You can enable your Apache server to use PHP by commanding **sudo apt-get install php5 libapache2-mod-php5 php5-mcrypt -y**.

You can also host Python programs as executable scripts by enabling CGI processing through Apache. Use the command **sudo a2enmod cgi**. Next, create a directory through which your site can access the .py files. To make all files in a CGI folder executable, use this configuration:

```
<Directory /srv/www/website/public_html/cgi-bin>
        Options ExecCGI
        SetHandler cgi-script
</Directory>
```

To allow .py files to be executable as scripts:

```
<Directory /srv/www/website/public_html>
        Options +ExecCGI
        AddHandler cgi-script .py
</Directory>
```

After that, you can compose a .py script and place it into one of these CGI-enabled folders, and it will be parsed and executed by Python 3.

By default, Apache will host a test page at your home IP address. From another computer, you can access your website at http://localhost/ or http:// followed by your own IP address.

Once your website is established, you will want to be able to control your system remotely, so this is another chance to use Putty to control the OS of your web server without touching it.

Chapter 6: Raspberry Pi Systems

The following examples in this section can be commanded through SSH.

You can see your server's IP address by commanding **hostname -I**. You can also set your own static IP address so that it will not change after the system reboots. Use the command **ifconfig** in the terminal to return your router information.

You will need to configure your network interface by using **sudo nano /etc/network/interfaces**, so take note of the following pieces of information. If you have a wired connection, note the part that says **eth0**. If you are on Wi-Fi, look at **wlan0**. You will need to remember **inet addr**, **Bcast**, and **Mask**. Finally, get your Gateway address by commanding **route -n**.

You will then change the network interface from **iface wlan0 inet dhcp** to:

Iface wlan0 inet static
address 000.000.0.0
netmask 000.000.0.0
gateway 000.000.0.0
network 000.000.0.0
broadcast 000.000.0.0

Put the previously noted information into their fields.

You may refresh your web server at will by commanding **sudo service apache2 restart**.

Your Own Robot

Who hasn't fantasized about an automaton that answers to our every whim and makes life a little bit easier? The advanced androids of our imagination may be a little far-fetched, but the Raspberry Pi can power a small, remotely controlled robot that can heft and transport small items. It's a good start.

Along with your RPI3 with Raspbian installed, you will need a few more parts to complete your first robot. The primary components are the robot chassis, an RTK Motor controller board, a Nintendo Wii remote, and a USB power pack. A chassis that moves the robot is available on Proto-PIC, the controller can be found on the Ryanteck website or The Pi Hit, and the Wii remote can come from any used game store.

The first thing that will be done is to attach the motor board to the Raspberry Pi 3 by plugging it into its GPIO pins. Be sure that the Pi has been cleanly shut down before adding any add-on boards. Connect the motors in the chassis to the motor board. Connect one motor to the connector marked J3/M1, and the other motor to J2/M2. Then, connect the battery pack to the control board so that you have a system that delivers signals to the motors when the Raspberry Pi commands it.

To test the motors, first **import RPi.GPIO as io** within a new Python file in the IDLE. Then, **import time**. Use the methods within those two modules to assign brief outputs to the GPIO pins connected to the motors and spin them each for just 0.5 seconds. To run the saved Python program, use **sudo python test_motors.py**.

To make your Nintendo Wii remote detectable by the Raspberry Pi 3's built-in Bluetooth, press the 1 and 2 buttons on the controller at the same time that you are scanning for devices. After you create a connection, command **sudo apt-get install python-cwiid**, which will install a Python module that will help you communicate to the Wii remote.

By using some code that is hosted on the Raspberry Pi website, you can quickly create the .py files that allow you to control the motors on a robot chassis. These are hosted at:

- https://www.raspberrypi.org/learning/robo-butler/code/robot.py

- https://www.raspberrypi.org/learning/robo-butler/code/wii_remote_1.py

Use **nano** to create text files named 'robot.py' and 'wii_remote_1.py' and copy / paste the code in the links into those text files. Commanding **sudo python wii_remote_1.py** will test the Wii remote and show if it is communicating with the Pi. By running the Python file with the command **sudo python robot.py**, you will gain control over your rover.

After following all of the procedures, and after some tuning and tinkering, you will have a robot that interprets commands from a Raspberry Pi, a Wii remote, and Python 3 code. Use your creativity and build a body for the robot. You can make it a cargo robot that lugs small objects, but you don't have to stop there. With more research and practice, you can enable your robot to light up, speak, and even interpret voice commands.

What will you do with the power of the Raspberry Pi 3?

Conclusion

Thanks again for taking the time to read this book!

You should now have a good understanding of how to use your Raspberry Pi and be ready to try out a few projects of your own!

If you enjoyed this book, please take the time to leave me a review on Amazon. I appreciate your honest feedback, and it really helps me to continue producing high quality books.